Psychoblessed

Anvikshaa Bisen

ISBN 978-93-5883-118-4
© Anvikshaa Bisen 2023

Published in India 2023 by Pencil

A brand of
One Point Six Technologies Pvt. Ltd.
Unit no. 26, Ground Floor, Building A1,
Wadala Truck Terminal Road,
Near Post Office, Antop Hill, Mumbai - 400037
E connect@thepencilapp.com
W www.thepencilapp.com

Author biography

I was born on 2nd May 2001 and completed my BSc Hons Psychology from Manipal University jaipur, I am passionate about understanding the intricacies of human behavior and contributing to the field of psychology. i got my psychological side from my mother, With a solid foundation in psychological theories and research methodologies, I am equipped to make a meaningful impact in various professional settings.During my academic journey, I have gained valuable knowledge in areas such as cognitive psychology, social psychology, developmental psychology, and research methods. I have developed strong analytical and critical thinking skills, allowing me to effectively analyze complex data and draw insightful conclusions.Complementing my theoretical knowledge.

My passion for helping others and making a positive difference has driven me to actively engage in volunteer work and internships related to mental health and well-being. These experiences have honed my interpersonal skills, empathy, and ability to work collaboratively in diverse teams.I am particularly interested in exploring areas such as neuropsychology, clinical psychology, and organizational psychology.

CONTENTS

AI in Virtual Reality Therapy

The incorporation of AI into virtual reality therapy holds the potential to transform the landscape of mental health interventions. AI-driven systems can analyze user data in real-time, including physiological responses, facial expressions, and verbal interactions, enabling personalized and adaptive virtual experiences. This real-time analysis allows AI algorithms to tailor the therapeutic scenarios based on individual responses, optimizing treatment outcomes and enhancing patient engagement. One key aspect of AI in virtual reality therapy is the ability to create personalized virtual environments that cater to the specific needs and preferences of each patient. The integration of AI in virtual reality therapy also raises important ethical considerations. Issues related to data privacy, informed consent, and the potential for harm to vulnerable populations require careful attention to ensure responsible and ethical use of AI technologies in mental health care.

VR and mental health

VR has extraordinary potential to help people overcome mental health problems if high levels of presence are achieved for situations that trouble them. Difficulties interacting in the world are at the heart of mental health issues [e.g. becoming highly anxious near spiders in arachnophobia, having intense flashbacks with reminders of past trauma in post-traumatic stress disorder (PTSD), fearing attack from people in persecutory delusions, resisting the urge to take another drink in alcohol abuse disorders]. Therefore recovery concerns thinking, reacting and behaving differently in these situations. The most successful interventions are those that enable people to make such changes in real-world situations. With VR, individuals can enter simulations of the difficult situations and be coached in the appropriate responses, based upon the best theoretical understanding of the specific disorder. The simulations can be graded in difficulty and repeatedly experienced until the right learning is made. Problematic situations difficult to find in real life can be realized at the flick of a switch. And the great advantage of VR is that individuals know that a computer environment is not real but their minds and bodies behave as if it is real; hence, people will much more easily face difficult situations in VR than in real life and be able to try out new therapeutic strategies. The learning can then transfer to the real world. For some disorders it may be possible to eradicate the need for any therapist input, while for other disorders the time required of skilled therapists could be greatly reduced. Thus VR could help improve access to the most effective psychological treatments. It may become the method of choice for psychological treatment: out with the couch, on with the headset.

There are also many other potential uses of VR in mental health. We originally set out seven purposes (Freeman, Reference Freeman2008): symptom assessment, identification of symptom markers or correlates, establishment of factors predictive of disorders, tests of putative causal factors, investigation of the differential prediction of symptoms, determination of toxic elements in the environment, and the development of treatment. For instance, standard mental health diagnosis chiefly comprises retrospective recall using clinician interview and validated questionnaires. Inevitably, human beings tend to be very subjective in their views. Memory, moreover, is notoriously fallible. In the clinic of the future, it is possible that problems could also be assessed live in VR. The technology could also help make substantial inroads into understanding the causes of mental health disorders, for example, pinpointing the environmental characteristics that raise the risk of adverse psychological reactions in the context of individual differences.

The aim of this paper is to highlight for clinicians and researchers in mental health the potential of VR technology. This includes a review of what has been learned empirically from the first generation of studies about the use of VR in assessing, understanding and treating the main adult mental health disorders. We wished to identify established findings, obvious areas of neglect and new directions of interest. These are the studies that have been conducted in specialist laboratories over the past 20 years, before the current transformation in availability and capabilities of the technology. It is the ambition of these pioneering studies that we aim to capture, as new hardware and software are dramatically altering what can be created in VR and the ease of use.

Personalizing Virtual Environment with AI

Data Collection and User Profiling:
AI-driven virtual reality therapy begins with the collection of relevant user data. Through various sensors and devices, such as eye-tracking technology, heart rate monitors, and facial expression analysis, AI systems can gather real-time data on a patient's physiological responses and emotional states during therapy sessions. This data is used to create a comprehensive user profile, which includes information about the individual's fears, triggers, stress levels, and emotional reactivity.

Real-Time Adaptation of Virtual Environments:
Based on the analysis of user data, AI can dynamically adapt the virtual environments to suit the individual's needs and preferences. For example, if a patient has a fear of heights, the AI system can gradually introduce height-related scenarios in the virtual environment, starting with mild exposures and progressively increasing the intensity based on the patient's comfort level.

Real-Time Feedback and Support:
During virtual reality therapy sessions, the AI system can provide real-time feedback and support to the patient. For instance, if the AI detects signs of heightened anxiety, it can offer coping strategies or relaxation techniques to help the patient manage their emotions and remain engaged in the therapeutic process.

Long-Term Progress Monitoring:
AI's ability to continuously analyze user data enables long-term progress monitoring. Therapists can access the AI-generated insights to assess the patient's improvement over time, allowing for data-driven decision-making in treatment planning and adjustments.

Benefits of Personalization:

The personalization of virtual environments through AI offers several advantages. Patients experience therapy that aligns precisely with their needs, increasing treatment efficacy and engagement. The adaptive nature of AI-driven virtual reality therapy can accelerate the therapeutic process and reduce the number of sessions required to achieve meaningful outcomes.

AI-Driven Behavioral Analysis

Real-Time Behavioral Assessment:
AI-driven behavioral analysis in virtual reality therapy involves the real-time assessment of a patient's behavior, responses, and interactions within the virtual environment. Through advanced sensors and data collection techniques, AI algorithms continuously monitor the patient's physiological signals, facial expressions, body language, and verbal interactions during therapy sessions.

Emotional Recognition:
AI-powered virtual reality therapy can recognize and interpret emotional cues exhibited by the patient. By analyzing facial expressions, tone of voice, and physiological responses (e.g., heart rate and sweating), the AI system can gauge the patient's emotional states, such as anxiety, fear, stress, or relaxation. This information helps in understanding the patient's emotional reactions to various scenarios and interventions.

Identifying Triggers and Patterns:
AI algorithms are capable of identifying triggers and patterns in the patient's behavior that may contribute to their mental health condition. For example, the AI may recognize specific situations or stimuli that consistently evoke fear or distress in the patient, helping therapists

pinpoint the root causes of their challenges.

Adaptive Therapy Interventions:

Based on the real-time behavioral analysis, AI can adapt therapy interventions to suit the patient's responses and needs. For instance, if the AI detects signs of heightened anxiety, it can modify the virtual environment or scenario to reduce stress levels and gradually expose the patient to challenging situations at a pace that matches their comfort level.

Progress Monitoring:

AI-driven behavioral analysis allows therapists to track the patient's progress and response to therapy over time. The data collected during each session can be aggregated and analyzed, providing valuable insights into the patient's treatment trajectory and identifying areas of improvement or stagnation.

AI-Driven Virtual Reality Therapy for Social Anxiety Disorder(SAD)

Background:

Social anxiety disorder (SAD) is a prevalent mental health condition characterized by intense fear and avoidance of social situations due to the fear of embarrassment, negative evaluation, or judgment. Traditional therapeutic approaches, such as cognitive-behavioral therapy (CBT) and exposure therapy, have shown effectiveness in treating SAD. However, some patients may find it challenging to engage in real-life exposure scenarios, limiting the effectiveness of these interventions.

Case Description:

A 30-year-old individual, named Alex, was diagnosed with severe social anxiety disorder. Alex's symptoms significantly impacted daily life, including avoiding social gatherings, public speaking situations, and even engaging in everyday conversations with strangers. Conventional therapy approaches did not lead to substantial progress, as Alex struggled with the real-life exposure exercises, causing discomfort and anxiety.

Intervention:

Alex was enrolled in a novel AI-driven virtual reality therapy program specifically designed for individuals with social anxiety disorder. The program utilized cutting-edge AI algorithms to personalize virtual environments and behavioral analysis to adapt therapy interventions.

AI-Driven Virtual Reality Therapy for Post Traumatic Stress Disorder(PTSD)

Background:

Post-Traumatic Stress Disorder (PTSD) is a debilitating mental health condition that can develop after exposure to traumatic events. Individuals with PTSD often experience distressing memories, flashbacks, nightmares, and heightened emotional arousal related to the traumatic event. Traditional therapeutic approaches, such as cognitive processing therapy (CPT) and eye movement desensitization and reprocessing (EMDR), have shown effectiveness in treating PTSD. However, some patients may struggle to engage fully in these therapies or may find it challenging to revisit traumatic memories in traditional settings.

Case Description:

Emma, a 34-year-old military veteran, was diagnosed with severe PTSD following her deployment to a conflict zone. Emma's symptoms included frequent nightmares, hypervigilance, and social withdrawal. Despite undergoing traditional therapy, Emma's progress was limited due to her resistance to revisiting traumatic memories and difficulties in fully engaging in exposure-based interventions.

Intervention:

Emma was offered participation in an AI-enhanced virtual reality therapy program designed specifically for individuals with PTSD. This cutting-edge program utilized artificial intelligence algorithms to personalize virtual environments and provide adaptive therapy interventions.

AI-Powered Virtual Reality Therapy for Fear of Flying

Background:

Fear of flying, also known as aviophobia, is a common specific phobia that affects a significant number of individuals worldwide. People with aviophobia experience intense anxiety and fear when boarding an aircraft or even thinking about flying. This fear can lead to avoidance of air travel, limiting career opportunities, and causing significant distress for those affected. Traditional therapeutic approaches, such as exposure therapy, have shown effectiveness in treating fear of flying. However, some individuals may find it difficult to engage fully in exposure exercises due to the real-life nature of the intervention.

Case Description:

John, a 42-year-old business executive, had been experiencing a severe fear of flying for several years. Despite the importance of air travel for his job, John had been avoiding flights altogether, which was negatively impacting his professional and personal life. He sought treatment to overcome his fear of flying and regain control over his travel-related anxiety.

Intervention:

John was enrolled in an innovative AI-powered virtual reality therapy program designed specifically for individuals with fear of flying. This program utilized advanced AI algorithms to create personalized virtual environments and deliver tailored therapeutic interventions.

AI-Driven Virtual Reality Therapy for Public Speaking Anxiety

Background:

Public speaking anxiety, also known as glossophobia, is a common social anxiety disorder characterized by intense fear and anxiety when speaking in front of an audience. Individuals with glossophobia may experience physical symptoms such as trembling, sweating, and rapid heartbeat, making public speaking a challenging and distressing experience. Traditional therapeutic approaches, such as cognitive-behavioral therapy (CBT) and exposure therapy, have shown effectiveness in treating public speaking anxiety. However, some individuals may find it difficult to engage fully in exposure exercises or may require additional support to overcome their fear.

Case Description:

Sarah, a 28-year-old marketing professional, had been struggling with severe public speaking anxiety for many years. Her fear of presenting in front of colleagues and clients was negatively impacting her career advancement and causing significant stress and self-doubt. Sarah sought help to improve her public speaking skills and overcome her anxiety.

Intervention:

Sarah was offered participation in an AI-driven virtual reality therapy program designed specifically to address public speaking anxiety. This cutting-edge program utilized advanced AI algorithms to personalize virtual environments and provide adaptive therapy interventions.

Addiction

Conditioned reactivity to drug-related cues is an important maintenance factor in drug and alcohol addiction, as such repeated exposure to drug-related cues has been used to reduce cue reactivity craving in order to prevent relapse. VR cue exposure provides the opportunity to conduct repeated exposures to drug-related cues in a controlled therapeutic environment. An initial pilot study found that VR-based cue exposure (e.g., a virtual bar, syringe, needle) was effective at eliciting physiological arousal, subjective craving, and urges to use drugs in men with opioid dependence.

Another investigation found that a VR "crack" cocaine environment was effective at eliciting craving and physiological arousal in a crack cocaine dependent sample A VR casino environment was shown to be effective in eliciting psychophysiological arousal and urges to gamble in a sample of recreational gamblers ,suggesting that VR based cue elicited craving is effective across different addiction populations. In a nicotine dependent sample, a VR-based smoking environment elicited increased psychophysiological arousal and craving compared to a neutral cue, and this response decreased over the course of a four week VR exposure treatment. In a sample of nicotine-dependent cigarette smokers, self-reported withdrawal symptoms and craving prior to a VR cue exposure were predictive of craving experienced in VR and significant increases in heart rate were present for three of the four VR smoking cues, providing further support for the ability of VR stimuli to effectively elicit subjective craving and physiological arousal related to substance-related cues. A double-blind placebo study investigated the effects of DCS in concurrent cocaine and nicotine-dependent participants (N=29) who engaged in VR based cue-exposure therapy in conjunction with brief cognitive-behavioral therapy for smoking. Results indicated no significant effect of DCS , however, overall significant decreases in smoking at mid and post-treatment compared to baseline and craving for cigarettes and cue-induced craving decreased over the course of the study. Notably, approximately 90% of the treatment sessions were attended, suggesting that VR based cue exposure therapy is a tolerable treatment approach. A randomized trial of CBT plus either smoking VR cue exposure therapy or placebo VR cue exposure therapy found that the smoking VR participants had a higher quit rate and reported significantly fewer cigarettes smoked per day at the end of treatment. As such, the extant literature suggests that VR-based environments are effective at eliciting cue reactivity and craving in different substance dependent populations and can be effectively incorporated within repeated cue exposure treatment.

Summary
AI in virtual reality therapy represents a groundbreaking and transformative approach to revolutionizing mental health interventions. The integration of AI-driven

behavioral analysis and personalization of virtual environments has the potential to significantly enhance the effectiveness and accessibility of mental health care. By continuously analyzing user data and recognizing emotional cues, AI can adapt therapy interventions in real-time, tailoring them to meet each individual's unique needs and challenges. The ability to create personalized virtual scenarios and provide real-time feedback empowers patients to confront fears, manage stress, and develop coping strategies in a controlled and safe environment.

However, the implementation of AI in virtual reality therapy is not without its challenges. Ethical considerations, including data privacy, informed consent, and bias mitigation, are critical to ensure the responsible and ethical use of AI technologies in mental health care. Striving for fairness and equitable care in AI-driven interventions is essential to avoid perpetuating existing disparities and providing equal opportunities for all patients. Moreover, standardization and interoperability remain crucial objectives to establish best practices and seamless integration of AI-driven virtual reality therapy into clinical settings. As the field evolves, collaboration between researchers, developers, therapists, and policymakers is vital to establish guidelines and ensure the effective and ethical implementation of AI-driven interventions.

Despite the challenges, the promise of AI in virtual reality therapy is immense. Through real-time behavioral analysis and continuous progress monitoring, therapists gain deeper insights into the patient's responses, enabling data-driven decision-making and personalized treatment plans.

In conclusion, AI-driven behavioral analysis and

personalized virtual environments offer a promising future for mental health care. As technology advances and ethical considerations are carefully addressed, AI in virtual reality therapy has the potential to empower patients, enhance therapy outcomes, and make mental health interventions more accessible to diverse populations.

Effect of Childhood Trauma in Romantic Relationship as in Expression of Love Language

Childhood trauma can cast a long shadow on one's life, affecting various aspects of their emotional and psychological well-being. One area profoundly influenced by early trauma is the way individuals express and interpret love in their romantic relationships. Love languages, popularized by Dr. Gary Chapman, encompass five primary modes of expressing affection: words of affirmation, acts of service, receiving gifts, quality time, and physical touch. This article explores how childhood trauma can impact the expression of love languages in romantic relationships, shedding light on the challenges couples may face and offering insights for healing and growth.

Childhood trauma can instill a deep-seated Fear of Intimacy and Vulnerability. Those who have endured traumatic experiences may struggle to let down their emotional barriers and embrace physical touch or quality time as expressions of love. Overcoming this fear requires patience, empathy, and a willingness to create a safe space within the relationship. Couples can work together to set boundaries and gradually build trust, allowing the survivor to feel more secure and comfortable in expressing and receiving affection.

Trauma can shatter a person's Ability to Trust others, leading them to question the sincerity behind acts of service and receiving gifts. Partners might encounter difficulties when trying to express love in these ways, as the survivor may doubt their intentions or feel unworthy of such gestures. In these cases, consistent support, understanding, and reassurance can aid in rebuilding trust and healing past wounds.

Childhood trauma often gives Rise to Coping Mechanisms that have lasting impacts on romantic relationships. For example, a survivor might develop self-sufficiency as a way to protect themselves from potential harm, hindering their ability to accept acts of service or help from their partner. Understanding the underlying reasons behind these coping mechanisms and recognizing their effects on love languages can aid in promoting healthier expressions of love within the relationship.

Attachment styles formed during childhood influence how individuals approach romantic relationships and love languages. Anxious Attachment Styles might lead individuals to seek constant reassurance through words of affirmation and quality time, while avoidant attachment styles might create a tendency to withdraw emotionally or avoid physical touch. Partners who understand each other's attachment styles can navigate these differences with empathy and patience.

By the style love language we can also predict their past childhood traumas:

- Words of Affirmation show lack of praise , no compliments, often criticized or judged.

- Quality time shows lack of attention often feeling lonely, alone, not seen or heard.

- Act of Service shows forced rom a young age to be independent.

- Physical touch shows lack of affection, discomfort in showing love.

- Gifts giving or receiving shows felt ignored or not noticed.

The impact of childhood trauma on love languages in romantic relationships is profound and complex. Recognizing the effects of trauma and being empathetic towards a partner's experiences are crucial steps in creating a supportive and nurturing environment for healing. By fostering open communication, patience, and understanding, couples can work together to overcome the challenges presented by childhood trauma and develop deeper, more fulfilling expressions of love in their relationship. Seeking professional therapy or counseling can also be immensely beneficial for both individuals, helping them navigate the journey towards healing and growth together.

Impact of toxic parenting in development of psychological disorders in adolescence and children in Indian context

Children and adolescents are highly influenced by their early environment, particularly the parenting they receive. Parenting styles and behaviors play a critical role in shaping a child's psychological development and well-being. However, when parenting practices become consistently negative, abusive, neglectful, or emotionally harmful, they can have detrimental effects on the mental health of children and adolescents. This phenomenon is known as "toxic parenting". In the Indian context, where cultural norms, values, and societal expectations significantly impact parenting practices, it is essential to examine the impact of toxic parenting on the development of psychological disorders in children and adolescents. India, with its diverse cultural landscape and unique parenting dynamics, presents a distinct context to explore the interplay between toxic parenting and psychological well-being.

The significance of this research lies in understanding how toxic parenting behaviors contribute to the manifestation and perpetuation of psychological disorders in Indian children and adolescents. By shedding light on this issue, it becomes possible to develop appropriate interventions and support systems to mitigate the long-term consequences of toxic parenting and promote healthier developmental outcomes.

The primary objective of this research paper is to comprehensively examine the impact of toxic parenting on the development of psychological disorders in children and adolescents within the Indian context. Specifically, the paper will explore prevalent psychological disorders among Indian youth and their association with toxic parenting behaviors. It will also analyze the cultural factors unique to India that influence toxic parenting practices.

According to a psychologist, Sri Juwita Kusumawardhani toxic parents are families who are unable to carry out family functions properly and are unable to provide a sense of security to their children. Mikulinser also explained that toxic parents are parents who adopt a lifestyle and also interactions that can damage the child's ability to build healthy relationships between families, as well as friends and partners. Meanwhile, according to Forward (1989) Toxic parents mean parents who harm, hurt and even harm their own children which lead to physical and psychological injuries that are embedded in children which can cause trauma.

According to Altridhonato, there are many factors that affects the quality of parenting on their children such as parental age, parental education, previous experience with child care, stress and relationship between husband and wife.

Every child is different and posses unique abilities that a parent should carefully understand and be considered of

.Understanding what triggers the childs anger and makes them sad and helping them overcome them by listening and understanding their problems and coming up with possible solutions to deal with it requires understanding, sympathy.

Dunham and Dermer (2011) Describe three types of toxic parents, namely: Contest parents, dismissive parents, and contemptuous parents who are insulting. Contest parents try to make children as they wish. Through the successes of the infant, this form of parent receives pseudo-self esteem. Parents encourage children to accept their wishes as child goals. The dismissive parent is not connected with children in the way intended. Parents may not be physically, emotionally, or financially available. Dismissive Parents may be in the house every day, but they are busy with their own lives and not involved in the children's lives. They may provide basic needs but without a warm emotional connection.

Prevalent Psychological Disorders in Indian Adolescents and Children

Psychological disorders among Indian adolescents and children are a significant concern that can have far-reaching consequences on their overall well-being and future prospects. Understanding the prevalent disorders is crucial for assessing the impact of toxic parenting on their development.

Following are the some psychological disorders:

Anxiety Disorders: Anxiety disorders, including generalized anxiety disorder (GAD), social anxiety disorder, and panic disorder, are prevalent among Indian youth. Excessive worry, fear, and avoidance behaviors can significantly impair daily functioning and academic performance.

Depression: Depression is a pervasive mental health issue affecting a substantial number of Indian adolescents and children. Persistent sadness, loss of interest, changes in sleep and appetite, and low self-esteem are common symptoms. The societal pressure to excel academically and the rapidly changing socio-cultural landscape contribute to the vulnerability of Indian youth to depression.

Attention-Deficit/Hyperactivity Disorder (ADHD): ADHD is characterized by difficulties in sustaining attention, hyperactivity, and impulsivity. It often leads to academic underachievement, impaired social relationships, and emotional dysregulation in Indian children and adolescents.

Eating Disorders: Although historically perceived as less prevalent in India, eating disorders like anorexia nervosa, bulimia nervosa, and binge eating disorder are increasingly being recognized. Societal pressures, body image issues, and cultural norms surrounding food and appearance contribute to the development of these disorders.

Substance Abuse Disorders: Substance abuse, particularly alcohol and tobacco, poses a significant problem among Indian adolescents. Peer influence, accessibility, and inadequate awareness about the consequences of substance abuse contribute to its prevalence.

Parenting Styles

There are many scholars obtain to define what parenting styles are. According to Adimora, D. E., Nwokenna, E. N., Omeje, J. C., & Umeano, E. C. (2015), parenting styles are the strategies used by parents for child-upgrading. It is characterized by the parents' responsiveness and demandingness, and also uninvolved style (Jinan, N., Mohmed Yusof, N. A. M., Vellasamy, V., Ahmad, A., Bin Abdul Rahman, M. N., & Motevalli, S. (2022). Furthermore, they explained that responsiveness of parents refers to parents' affection toward the children, talk, support and reason while the demandingness refers to parents' control, authority and norms created for the children. The parenting style then categorised based on the level of parents' responsiveness, demands and uninvolved in child- rearing efforts. Furthermore, Jinan, N, et all (2022) stated that there are 4 parenting style.

Parents play the role as the controller after having a dialogue what children interest about. The third, the permissive parenting style in which children get more parents' responsiveness with less demandingness

Toxic Parenting: Definition and Types

No one is perfect, including our parents. Parents are human beings too. They may have the best intentions and want the best for their children, but they make mistakes and might unintentionally do damaging things at times. Despite this, their impulse is to do better, improve, and make things right.

Toxic parenting, however, involves parents who carry a promise of love and care, but at the same time, mistreat their children. They partake in parenting styles that inflict on-going and repetitive trauma, abuse, humiliation, and ill-will. They don't treat their children with respect as individuals, compromise, take responsibility for their behavior, nor are they likely to apologize. They lack compassion and nurturing abilities and are more concerned with their own needs than worrying about whether or not what they are doing is harmful or damaging.

This repeated behavior creates fear, guilt, obligation, and leaves a child with emotional scars. Toxic parents treat their children in ways that make them doubt their importance, self-worth, and make them question if they are worthy of love, approval, and validation. Scared by loud noises , instant crying when yelled at ,constantly apologising,isolating oneself when upset, Healing makes you lose interest in many things you once connected with.Not even out if sadness, but from finally seeing people and things for who and what they really are.

Types of Toxic Parents

- The godlike parents– suffocate their child's independence to the point that the child can't survive on their own. This environment encourages the belief that the child is bad and weak and the parents are good and strong.

- The inadequate parents– these parents focus on their own survival; the child becomes almost invisible and is forced to grow up fast. As a result, these children find it difficult to develop a sense of self-worth.

- The controllers– these parents try to live vicariously through their children and control their lives even in adulthood. These children develop anxious and fearful personalities and have difficulties maturing. These parents often use guilt and shame to leverage themselves.

- The verbal abusers– these parents directly insult their children or are cynical and sarcastic to intentionally hurt their feelings and put them down. You often see this parenting style in extremely competitive people or perfectionist parents who are never satisfied with anything. This results in the child internalizing and starting to believe what their parents say about them.

- The physical abusers– physical abuse often happens because of the parent's exhaustion, high stress levels, anxiety, their own unhappiness and lack of impulse control, or because physical abuse was normal for them as they grew up. These parents lash out when their children don't meet their needs. This parent style results in feelings of rage, revenge fantasies, and self-hatred in the children.

- The active abuser– physically abuses the child

- The passive abuser– they witness the abuse but do nothing to protect the child. Results in a form of abandonment.

- The alcoholics– they do everything mentioned above. Drinking also leads to a destruction of vulnerability, trust, and openness. The child becomes a scapegoat for all that is wrong with the parent and they learn early on that relationships lead to betrayal and love leads to pain.

- The sexual abusers– the ultimate betrayal. Destroys the child's innocence and leads to them feeling dirty, damaged, and different. The children are robbed of healthy relationships and sexuality.

Changes in Personality due to Toxic Parenting

- Toxic parenting behaviors have a profound impact on a child's personality development. The consistent exposure to negative, abusive, or neglectful parenting practices can lead to significant changes in a child's personality traits and behavioral patterns. The following are some key changes in personality that may occur due to toxic parenting:

- Low Self-Esteem: Toxic parenting often involves criticism, belittlement, and constant negative reinforcement. Children growing up in such an environment may develop low self-esteem and a negative self-perception. They may doubt their abilities, feel unworthy, and struggle with self-confidence.

- Fearfulness and Anxiety: Toxic parenting can create an atmosphere of fear and anxiety for the child. Frequent yelling, threats, or physical abuse can make children constantly on edge and hyper-vigilant. As a result, they may develop heightened anxiety levels, exhibiting signs of fearfulness, social withdrawal, and a constant need for reassurance.

- Aggression and Hostility: Children who experience toxic parenting may display increased aggression and hostility in their behavior. They may internalize the anger and frustration they feel due to the negative treatment they receive and express it towards others through verbal or physical aggression.

- Emotional Instability: Toxic parenting can disrupt the development of emotional regulation skills in children. They may struggle to manage and express their emotions appropriately, leading to emotional instability. This instability can manifest as frequent mood swings, difficulty controlling anger, or emotional outbursts.

- Trust Issues and Attachment Problems: Consistent exposure to toxic parenting can erode trust in relationships. Children may develop trust issues, fearing betrayal or rejection. They may also struggle with forming healthy attachments and maintaining secure relationships due to their experiences of neglect, abuse, or inconsistent caregiving.

- Perfectionism and Need for Control: Toxic parenting can instill a sense of constant pressure and perfectionism in children. They may develop a strong need for control as a coping mechanism to navigate unpredictable and hostile environments. This drive for control can manifest as excessive self-criticism, fear of failure, and difficulty in adapting to change.

- Social Withdrawal and Isolation: Children who experience toxic parenting may become socially withdrawn and isolated. They may struggle with forming and maintaining healthy relationships, fearing rejection or judgment from others. The negative experiences at home may make them hesitant to engage in social interactions and develop trust in peers or authority figures.

How to Heal from Toxic Parenting

- Healing comes from a place of understanding. I know that it can be difficult to "unlearn" the toxic patterns of behaviors that you grew up around, but you can overcome them. You can eventually separate yourself from your parents, change yourself for the better, and set boundaries that work for you.

- Become aware of your true feelings, beliefs, and behaviors towards your parents

- Rather than use forgiveness as an excuse that it didn't happen, actively grieve

- Grief lets you get unstuck, allows you to heal, and enables you to do something about your lost childhood

- Make it clear that your parents' toxic behaviors were not your responsibility

- Give yourself permission to be angry, without making any judgements

- Talk about your anger with safe people, increase your physical activity, use your anger as a source of self-definition for you to define your limits and boundaries

- Gain emotional independence

- Allow yourself to be who you are and let your parents be who they are

- Proactively communicate and confront your parents if necessary

- If you choose to confront your parents, do it for yourself, not for them. Simply having the courage to do it is successful. Your response is what matters, not their reaction to the confrontation

- Break the cycle and try your best to not impose toxicity onto your own children

Summary

Toxic parenting in the Indian context has significant implications for the development of psychological disorders and changes in personality among children and adolescents. This research paper has examined the impact of toxic parenting on the mental health and well-being of Indian youth, highlighting the prevalence of psychological disorders such as anxiety, depression, ADHD, conduct disorders, eating disorders, and substance abuse.

The findings demonstrate that toxic parenting practices, characterized by negativity, abuse, neglect, and emotional harm, contribute to the manifestation and perpetuation of these psychological disorders. The consistent exposure to toxic parenting leads to changes in personality, including low self-esteem, fearfulness, aggression, emotional instability, trust issues, perfectionism, and social withdrawal. Cultural factors unique to India, such as societal expectations, parenting styles, and gender dynamics, also play a role in influencing toxic parenting behaviors. The cultural context must be taken into consideration when developing interventions and support systems to address toxic parenting and promote healthier developmental outcomes.

Interventions and support systems are crucial in mitigating the long-term effects of toxic parenting. Early intervention, involving mental health professionals, schools, and community-based programs, is essential to provide children and adolescents with the necessary tools and support to overcome the challenges they face due to toxic parenting. This research paper emphasizes the importance of raising awareness about toxic parenting in India, encouraging further research, and advocating for policy changes to address this critical issue. By recognizing the impact of toxic parenting on the mental well-being of Indian youth, we can work towards creating a nurturing and supportive environment that fosters healthy development and resilience in children and adolescents.

In conclusion, addressing toxic parenting and its impact on psychological disorders and personality changes in Indian youth requires a multi-faceted approach involving families, communities, schools, and policymakers. By promoting positive parenting practices, providing accessible mental health services, and creating supportive environments, we can empower children and adolescents to overcome the challenges associated with toxic parenting and achieve optimal mental well-being.

Examining the Impact of Covid-19 on Eating Preferences

The Covid-19 pandemic, which was an unprecedent global crisis which affected various aspects of human life and was responsible for killing millions of people worldwide as it was a virus and its basic characteristic was mutation which was essential for its survival in the host and for this reason scientists could not find the cure for this deadly disease and hence vaccination was ineffective.

It caused a sudden change in immediate health and economic impact which played a factor in influencing food preferences. The measures implemented to prevent the spread of the virus such as travel restriction, social distancing and lockdown which significantly changed peoples daily routine and access to food. The fear and uncertainty which aroused due to this pandemic paid a significant role in how people adjust to this new lifestyle and cope with stress and hence consume the food.

This research paper aims to provide a comprehensive analysis of the effects of the Covid-19 pandemic on food habits and preferences. It examines the changes observed in food consumption patterns, dietary habits, and food preferences during and after the pandemic, considering both short-term and potential long-term consequences. The pandemic has brought about various disruption in food consumption patterns. The food supply chain was strongly impacted in the early stages of the pandemic due to panic buying and stockpiling of food items.

Moreover, the pandemic has had an impact on dietary habits and nutritional choices. The stress and uncertainty associated with the crisis have led to emotional eating and increased snacking, potentially contributing to less balanced diets. The limitations on eating out and the fear of contagion have also affected individuals' choices regarding restaurant food, with a shift towards home-cooked meals.

Changes in Food Consumption habits

The Covid-19 pandemic has had a profound impact on our day to day routines, including food consumption habits. At the onset of the pandemic, there was a surge in panic buying and stockpiling of essential food items. Consumers rushed to grocery stores, resulting in shortages and imbalances in the food supply chain. Staple items such as rice, pasta, canned goods, and cleaning supplies experienced high demand, leading to temporary scarcity in some regions. The pandemic has influenced people's choices regarding the types of food they consume. With increased time spent at home and limited access to dining out options, individuals have turned to more shelf-stable and long-lasting foods. Non-perishable items, frozen foods, and canned goods have become more popular due to their extended shelf life and ease of storage. Additionally, there has been a rise in the consumption of comfort foods and indulgent snacks as people seek emotional comfort during these challenging times. The closure of restaurants and restrictions on dining out have led to a significant increase in home cooking and baking. With more time spent at home, individuals have taken up cooking as a way to pass the time, experiment with new recipes, and engage in creative culinary pursuits. he pandemic has heightened awareness of health and wellbeing, leading to an increased emphasis on consuming foods perceived as healthy and immune-boosting.

Dietary Habits and Nutritional Changes

The Covid-19 pandemic has had a significant impact on dietary habits and nutritional choices. : The disruption caused by the pandemic has influenced individuals' ability to maintain balanced diets. Stress, anxiety, and changes in daily routines have led to irregular eating patterns and disrupted meal schedules. Many people have reported emotional eating and increased snacking as a way to cope with the uncertainty and stress associated with the pandemic. The confinement and emotional strain of the pandemic have contributed to an increase in snacking and emotional eating. People often turn to food for comfort during times of stress, which can lead to excessive consumption of energy-dense, nutrient-poor foods. The proximity to the kitchen and easy access to snacks at home have further facilitated this behaviour. Emotional eating and snacking can contribute to weight gain and an imbalanced nutrient intake.

Factors affecting food preferences
Psychological Factors: The pandemic has brought about increased stress, anxiety, and emotional upheaval for many individuals. Psychological factors, such as comfort-seeking, boredom, and the need for emotional support, can

significantly impact food preferences. Comfort foods, which are often associated with positive emotions and nostalgia, have gained popularity as people seek solace and familiarity during challenging times. Additionally, boredom and monotony may lead to a desire for novelty, prompting individuals to try new recipes or explore different cuisines.

Health Concerns and Immune-Boosting Foods: The heightened focus on health and well-being during the pandemic has influenced food preferences. Individuals are more conscious of their immune system's role in fighting infections, leading to an increased interest in foods believed to boost immunity. There is a growing preference for fruits, vegetables, whole grains, lean proteins, and foods rich in vitamins, minerals, and antioxidants. People are actively seeking out foods that support their overall health and enhance their immune function.

Sustainability and Ethical Considerations: The pandemic has highlighted the interconnectedness between human health, animal welfare, and the environment. This awareness has influenced food preferences, with individuals showing a greater interest in sustainable and ethical food options. There is a growing demand for locally sourced, organic, and environmentally friendly foods. Consumers are considering factors such as carbon footprint, animal welfare standards, and support for local farmers and producers when making food choices.

Access to Food and Availability: The availability and accessibility of food have a significant impact on food preferences during the pandemic. Disruptions in the food supply chain, temporary shortages, and limited access to certain food items have influenced what people choose to consume. Individuals may opt for alternative ingredients or substitute their preferred choices based on what is readily available. Economic factors also play a role, as affordability and budget constraints may shape food preferences.

Social and Cultural Influences: Social and cultural influences continue to shape food preferences during the pandemic. Social media platforms, online communities, and virtual interactions have become avenues for sharing recipes, food trends, and recommendations. These platforms influence individuals' choices by exposing them to new ideas and food experiences. Cultural traditions and family practices also influence food preferences, as individuals may seek comfort in familiar foods or engage in cooking practices that reflect their cultural heritage.

Long term effects and implications

The Covid-19 pandemic has the potential to bring about long-term effects and implications for food habits and preferences. Understanding these effects is essential for anticipating shifts in behaviour and addressing the broader implications they may have on public health, food systems, and sustainability. The following are some potential long-term effects and their implications:

Changes in Dietary Preferences: The pandemic has disrupted established food habits and preferences, leading to potential long-term changes in dietary preferences. Increased home cooking, reliance on shelf-stable and long-lasting foods, and a greater emphasis on health and nutrition may persist beyond the pandemic. People may continue to prioritize cooking meals from scratch, incorporating more fruits and vegetables into their diets, and seeking out foods that support their immune systems.

Implication: This presents an opportunity to promote healthier eating habits and support sustainable food choices. Public health campaigns, educational initiatives, and food industry efforts can focus on promoting nutritious and sustainable food options that align with the changed dietary preferences.

Heightened Awareness of Food Safety and Hygiene: The pandemic has heightened public awareness of food safety and hygiene practices. People have become more conscious of the importance of proper food handling, cleanliness, and sanitization. This increased awareness is likely to influence food preferences and consumption behaviours in the long term, with individuals being more cautious about the sources and preparation of their food.

Implication: The food industry will need to adapt and prioritize food safety and hygiene practices to meet the expectations of consumers. Enhanced regulations, certifications, and transparency in the food supply chain can help build trust and ensure the long-term safety and quality of the food consumed.

Shifts in Sustainable Food Choices: The pandemic has brought sustainability and ethical considerations to the forefront of discussions around food choices. Individuals have shown an increased interest in local and seasonal foods, support for small-scale farmers and producers, and a desire to reduce their environmental footprint. This shift towards sustainable food choices may continue as people become more conscious of the environmental impact of their dietary decisions.

Implication: The food industry can respond to this shift by prioritizing sustainable practices, such as reducing food waste, adopting eco-friendly packaging, and promoting regenerative agriculture. Encouraging local food systems, community-supported agriculture, and providing clear information about the origin and sustainability of food products can further support this trend.

Strategies for promoting healthy and sustainable eating
We must promote healthy and sustainable eating for the long-term sustainability of our food systems and for our individual well-being. Keeping our food systems sustainable and healthy is crucial for individual well-being and our long-term well-being. Our food systems must be sustained long-term by promoting sustainable and healthy eating. Healthy eating is essential to individual well-being as well as long-term food sustainability. In order to ensure the long-term sustainability of our food systems, it is crucial that we promote healthy and sustainable eating. Healthy and sustainable eating is crucial to individuals' well-being and the sustainability of the food system. Healthy eating and sustainable food systems are essential to individual well-being and long-term food system sustainability. Our food systems and individual well-being rely on the promotion of sustainable and healthy diets.

- Public Health Campaigns: Develop and implement public health campaigns that raise awareness about the importance of healthy eating and sustainable food choices. These campaigns can provide information on the benefits of consuming a balanced diet, highlight the environmental impact of food choices, and promote local and seasonal produce.

- Nutrition Education: Provide comprehensive nutrition education in schools, community centres, and healthcare settings. Teach individuals about the importance of nutrient-rich foods, portion control, and mindful eating. Empower individuals to make informed choices by providing them with practical knowledge on reading food labels, meal planning, and cooking healthy meals.

- Sustainable Food Systems: Support and invest in sustainable agriculture practices that prioritize soil health, water conservation, and biodiversity. Encourage the use of regenerative farming techniques that restore and enhance the natural resources used in food production. Promote local and regional food systems to reduce the carbon footprint associated with long-distance transportation.

- Food Waste Reduction: Implement initiatives to reduce food waste throughout the supply chain and at the consumer level. Encourage proper food storage, meal planning, and creative ways to utilize leftovers. Support food recovery programs that redirect surplus food to those in need.

- Behavioural Nudges: Utilize behavioural science techniques to nudge individuals towards healthier and sustainable food choices. This can include strategies such as placing healthier options prominently in food environments, utilizing appealing signage and visuals, and making sustainable choices the default option in cafeterias and food delivery platforms.

- Policy and Regulation: Advocate for policies that support healthy and sustainable eating. This can include implementing taxes on unhealthy foods, restricting the marketing of unhealthy products to children, and providing incentives for sustainable farming practices.

Summary

The Covid-19 pandemic has brought about significant changes in food habits and preferences, with potential long-term effects and implications. The shifts observed in dietary choices, such as increased home cooking, emphasis on health and immune-boosting foods, and a greater focus on sustainability, provide opportunities for promoting healthier and more sustainable eating habits. Addressing these changes requires a multi-faceted approach. Public health campaigns, nutrition education, and improved food labeling and transparency can empower individuals to make informed choices aligned with their health and sustainability goals. Ensuring access to healthy food in underserved communities and collaborating with the food industry to offer healthier options are crucial steps toward creating a supportive food environment.

Promoting sustainable food systems, reducing food waste, and supporting regenerative agriculture practices are essential for building a resilient and environmentally friendly food system. Embracing digital technologies while addressing digital inequalities can enhance access to diverse food options and knowledge-sharing platforms.

It is evident that a comprehensive strategy is needed to promote healthy and sustainable eating in the post-pandemic era. By implementing strategies that encompass education, accessibility, collaboration, and policy changes, we can work towards a future where individuals are empowered to make choices that benefit their well-being, the environment, and the sustainability of our food systems.

Can Socialization reduce the chances of Drug Abuse

Drug abuse is a pervasive societal issue that has numerous detrimental effects on individuals and communities. Finding effective strategies to prevent drug abuse is crucial for promoting healthier lifestyles and reducing the associated social, economic, and health consequences. Socialization, the process of interacting and engaging with others in various social settings, has been recognized as a potentially influential factor in mitigating the risks of drug abuse. This article explores the relationship between socialization and drug abuse, highlighting how socialization can help reduce the chances of drug abuse.

The Importance of Socialization: Socialization plays a critical role in human development, shaping behaviors, attitudes, and beliefs from early childhood through adulthood. Positive socialization involves the acquisition of social skills, empathy, and a sense of belonging, which contribute to healthy relationships and overall well-being. Engaging in social activities and maintaining strong connections with family, friends, and community members can significantly impact an individual's choices and behaviors, including the decision to avoid drug abuse.

Protective Factors of Socialization:

- Social Support: A strong social support network provides individuals with emotional assistance, guidance, and reinforcement of positive behavior. It acts as a protective factor against drug abuse by offering individuals a sense of belonging and a support system during challenging times.

- Peer Influence: Peers have a substantial influence on behavior, particularly during adolescence when susceptibility to risky behaviors such as drug abuse is heightened. Positive peer influence, facilitated through socialization, can help promote healthy behaviors and discourage drug use.

- Healthy Activities: Engaging in social activities, sports, hobbies, and community events provides individuals with meaningful alternatives to drug use. These activities foster a sense of purpose, personal growth, and positive social connections, reducing the likelihood of turning to drugs as a source of stimulation or escape.

- Education and Awareness: Socialization within educational settings can provide valuable information and knowledge about the risks and consequences of drug abuse. Peer-led prevention programs, discussions, and awareness campaigns can effectively raise awareness and promote informed decision-making among young individuals.

- Positive Role Models: Socialization offers opportunities to interact with positive role models, such as parents, teachers, mentors, and community leaders, who can provide guidance, support, and inspiration. These role models can help shape individuals' attitudes and behaviors, including discouraging drug abuse.

Socialization plays a crucial role in reducing the chances of drug abuse by providing individuals with a support network, positive role models, and healthy alternatives. By fostering strong social connections, promoting positive peer influence, and increasing awareness about the risks of drug abuse, socialization can contribute to healthier lifestyles and drug-free communities. It is essential for families, communities, and educational institutions to recognize the power of socialization and implement strategies that encourage and facilitate positive social interactions, ultimately helping individuals make healthier choices and reduce the likelihood of drug abuse.

Role of Mental Health in Sports

Sports have long been a realm of physical prowess, technical skills, and competitive spirit, where athletes push their limits to achieve greatness. However, beneath the surface of athletic prowess lies a crucial yet often overlooked factor that profoundly impacts an athlete's success and well-being: mental health. The interplay between mental and physical aspects of sports is increasingly gaining recognition, as researchers, athletes, and sports professionals realize the significance of mental well-being in optimizing performance and promoting a healthy sporting environment.

Psychology is the systematic and scientific study of behavior and mental processes. Behaviors are the observable actions and responses given by humans and animals. They might include eating, laughing, drinking, sleeping etc. Mental processes are not directly visible and they include more abstract processes such as thinking, imaging, studying, learning, dreaming etc. Wilhelm Wundt is known as the father of psychology and he established the first lab of psychology at the University of Leipzig in Germany in 1879. In India, the first lab of psychology was established by N.N. Sengupta in 1915 at the University of Calcutta.

Sport is defined by Loy(1969) as an institutionalised, competitive game occurrence characterized by physical prowess, strategy and chance in combination. The history of sports is an old one and dates as far back as 70000 BC. The physical activity that developed into sports had early links with warfare and entertainment according to Crowther, Nigel B.(2007). Cave paintings of Lascaux caves in France seem to depict wrestling and sprinting, they are dated to be as old as 15,300 years old as told by Capelo, Holly (July 2010).

From the 1890s until his death in 1939, the Austrian physician Sigmund Freud developed psychoanalysis, a method of investigation of the mind and the way one thinks; a systematized set of theories about human behaviour; and a form of psychotherapy to treat psychological or emotional distress, especially unconscious conflict. Freud's psychoanalytic theory was largely based on interpretive methods, introspection and clinical observations. It became very well-known, largely because it tackled subjects such as sexuality, repression, and the unconscious mind as general aspects of psychological development. These were largely considered taboo subjects at the time, and Freud provided a catalyst for them to be openly discussed in polite society.

There is a wide consensus among historians that modern sports, particularly team sports originated in Europe and according to Bernard Lewis is a part of Western culture. An article written in The New York Times described that traditional team sports are seen as springing primarily from Britain and with the spread of the British empire they were taken to various parts of the world. The empire dissolved but the culture of sports still persists around the world. The most famous games that were spread around the world with their roots in colonialism are Cricket and Football, both were exported from Britain by Britain and initially for Britain. Cricket was seen as a game for aristocracy and football was viewed as a game for the working class and peasants. Regardless of the origins of the game, the Industrial Revolution and mass manufacturing brought increased leisure, which allowed more time to be spent playing or watching (and gambling on) spectator sports, as well as less elitism and greater accessibility to sports of all types. Professionalism in sports grew with the development of mass media and global communication, which increased sports popularity in general.

The experiment conducted by Triplett in 1890 on the phenomenon of social facilitation gave rise to the field of sport psychology. Then in 1925, Coleman Griffith created the Athletic Research Laboratory at the University of Illinois.

The application of the science of mind and behaviour to the field of sport has not been seen much in India, it is still in the developing phase or one can even say in its nascent stage. The first use of science comes in the form of journals being published about it in the 1960s and 70s. The founding of the Indian Association of Sports Medicine (IASM) in 1970 marks the beginning of the major development of the Indian sports science movement. Another significant milestone for sports psychology in India occurred in 1977, during the IASM's seventh annual conference when certain IASM delegates interested in the psychological aspects of sports joined together to form their own group. This is the idea behind the Indian Association of Sports Psychology. Many other institutes and groups, such as the Sport Psychology Association of India (SAPI), have been established over the years to aid in the development of sports psychology in the country (Anoushka Thakkar 2019).

According to a study conducted by the US Department of Health and Studies in 2012, they concluded that the prevalence of mental health issues in the USA was 1 in every 5 individuals (20%) and this rate increased when it was tested for individuals aged between 18 to 25 to 30%. When looking for similar studies conducted in India it was found that there has been no solid study on the matter and no data has been published by the concerned authority, and what little exists is in the form of low-quality research demonstrating non-rigorous research methods (Thomas McCabe et. al 2021).

Raglin (2001) states that the Mental health model of sports performance was given by Morgan in the 1980s and it postulates that there exists an inverse relationship between sports performance and mental health, whenever the psychopathology of an athlete is affected the performance of the athlete falls and rises accordingly. There are studies that say that Morgan overemphasized the role of psychopathology in sports performance (Vealey rs) and that psychotherapy may actually be counterproductive to sports performance (Danish sj) however research with the Olympic skiing team concluded that depression leads to a decrease in the performance of the athletes and studies like these works to solidify the main point of MHM hence strengthening the argument put forward by MHM (Raglin 2001)

In Silva and Weinberg's (1984) text, sport psychology was defined more broadly as either a concern for "the effect of psychological factors on behaviour in sport or the psychological effect that participation in sport or physical activity has on the performer". Sports psychology covers a large area from performance under pressure to confidence to conflict management and everything in between. When indulged in sports on a professional level, not only are they under the pressure to perform well in their games and matches but there is also a whole web of other related issues, psychological and sociological in nature working behind them in cohorts for them to reach there, these may come in the form of effective relationship management with theory partner, maintaining friendships and social circles, developing and evolving a healthy relationship with their peers, handling the fame sustaining hardships and maintaining efforts over long periods of time and sometimes these efforts don't yield the desired results so than finding the strength to still keep going.

Use of Psychological skills in Sports

- Psychological skills have long been acknowledged as being a critical component for athletes to perform at peak levels and to achieve the status of elites. Athletes are required to be mentally resilient to be successful. Mental toughness or resilience provides a new aspect to the already established norm of genetic giftedness. A player capable of mastering their emotion is taken to have a good mindset for winning the game. Emotional intelligence which is the mental capacity of a person to self-motivate, regulate, be self-aware, empathise and maintain interpersonal relations can be taken as a determinant of success as a team player and to possess leadership qualities. These skills are not limited to physical abilities but encompass the mental aspect of the game, empowering athletes to perform at their best in both training and competitive environments.

- Psychological Skills commonly used in Sports:-

- Goal Setting: Goal setting is a fundamental psychological skill used by athletes to establish clear and specific objectives. By setting short-term and long-term goals, athletes can focus their efforts, track progress, and stay motivated. Effective goal setting helps athletes prioritize their training and competition strategies, leading to improved performance.

- Visualization: Visualization, also known as mental imagery, involves mentally rehearsing sports-related scenarios in vivid detail. Athletes visualize successful performances, skill execution, and achieving their goals. This technique helps enhance confidence, improve concentration, and reduce anxiety, as the brain perceives imagined experiences similarly to real ones.

- Self-Talk: Positive self-talk involves using affirmations, motivational statements, and constructive internal dialogue. By replacing negative thoughts with encouraging and supportive self-talk, athletes can boost confidence, regulate emotions, and maintain focus during high-pressure situations.

- Relaxation Techniques: Stress and anxiety are common in sports, especially during competitions. Athletes use relaxation techniques like deep breathing, progressive muscle relaxation, and meditation to calm their nerves and regain composure. These techniques help reduce muscle tension and promote a state of mental and physical relaxation.

- Concentration and Focus: Maintaining focus is critical for consistent performance. Athletes use attentional control techniques to concentrate on relevant cues, block out distractions, and stay in the present moment. Focused attention is essential for making quick decisions and executing precise movements during sports.

- Pre-Performance Routines: Pre-performance routines involve a series of actions or rituals that athletes follow before competitions or crucial events. These routines create a sense of familiarity and predictability, reducing anxiety and enhancing mental readiness for performance.

- Team Communication: Effective communication within a team is a psychological skill that fosters collaboration and cohesion. Athletes use verbal and non-verbal communication to coordinate strategies, provide support, and foster a positive team environment.

Case Studies and Interviews

We will understand the role of mental health in sports by case studies of sports person

Michael Johnson

In 1997, Johnson faced a significant setback when he suffered a hamstring injury just weeks before the World Championships. Johnson remained steadfast in his determination. He worked closely with sports psychologists to develop mental strategies to cope with the pressure and uncertainty. He focused on visualization techniques, picturing himself crossing the finish line with his characteristic speed and grace. By visualizing success and focusing on his strengths, Johnson maintained a positive mindset. Through intensive physical therapy and unwavering mental toughness, Johnson made a remarkable recovery and competed in the World Championships. Not only did he participate, but he also went on to win the 400 meters event, showcasing his exceptional mental strength and resilience.

Serena Williams

As one of the greatest tennis players of all time, provides an excellent case study of the significant role of psychological skills in sports. Throughout her illustrious career, Serena's mental fortitude and resilience have been instrumental in her dominance on the tennis court. Her mental resilience, confidence, and mental preparation have allowed her to win numerous Grand Slam titles and maintain her status as one of the most dominant forces in women's tennis. Her unwavering focus on mental well-being and mental preparation underscores the significance of the mental aspect in achieving and sustaining excellence in sports.

Michael Phelps

He most decorated Olympian in history with 28 Olympic medals (23 of them gold), provides a compelling case study of the critical role of psychological skills in sports. Throughout his swimming career, Phelps demonstrated exceptional mental fortitude and utilized various psychological techniques to optimize his performance. His unwavering focus on mental preparation, goal setting, visualization, emotional regulation, and self-confidence propelled him to unparalleled success in the pool.

LeBron James

A basketball superstar, provides an exemplary case study of the vital role of mental toughness and leadership in sports, specifically in basketball. Throughout his illustrious NBA career, James has consistently demonstrated exceptional mental fortitude and leadership qualities, which have played a significant role in his success and impact on the game. His unwavering self-belief, resilience, emotional regulation, focus, and adaptability have been key factors in his extraordinary success on the court.

Dr. Sarah Collins

A seasoned sports psychologist, shares valuable insights into the significance of mental health in sports:

Q: How does mental health impact an athlete's performance?

Mental health plays a critical role in an athlete's performance. It affects their ability to handle pressure, stay focused, and make split-second decisions during competitions. When athletes are mentally strong, they can approach challenges with a positive mindset, which can lead to improved performance and consistency.

Q: What strategies do you recommend to athletes for managing stress and anxiety?

Stress and anxiety are common in sports, but there are effective strategies to manage them. I often advise athletes to practice relaxation techniques, such as deep breathing or progressive muscle relaxation, to calm their nerves. Additionally, encouraging athletes to maintain a routine and stay organized can help reduce anxiety before competitions.

Q: How can athletes build and maintain self-confidence?

Building self-confidence is a process that requires consistent effort. Athletes can work on their confidence by setting realistic goals and celebrating small achievements along the way. Positive self-talk and affirmations are also powerful tools in boosting self-confidence.

Q: What role does team dynamics play in an athlete's mental well-being?

Team dynamics significantly impact an athlete's mental well-being. A supportive and positive team environment fosters camaraderie and motivation. However, unresolved conflicts or negative team dynamics can lead to stress and affect an athlete's focus and performance.

Q: How can sports organizations better support athletes' mental health?

Sports organizations should prioritize mental health by providing access to sports psychologists and mental health professionals. Education and awareness programs can also help reduce the stigma surrounding mental health issues in sports, encouraging athletes to seek help when needed.

Benefits of Participation in Sports

Participation in sports is important to all people furthermore it has been found that participation in sports leads to various benefits in all facets of life be it psychological, physical or social (Danish 2005). It has been found that exercise can help reduce the chances of occurrence of serious mental illness, in a study conducted by Fox, K(2000) it was found that regular participation in sports leads to a decreased chances of depression, it also helps reduce symptoms of anxiety in the short term and help reduce the tendencies of anxiety in the long run simultaneously they also found that participation in sports help reduce stress and also building resilience in individuals. All these factors combine together to help battle the risk of development of any serious mental illness, so mere participation in sports helps individuals tackle the risk of developing mental illness.

Summary

The case studies of athletes like Michael Phelps, Michael Johnson, Serena Williams and LeBron James underscore the critical role of mental health and psychological skills in sports. These remarkable athletes exemplify how mental resilience, goal setting, visualization, emotional regulation, and effective leadership can significantly impact performance, well-being, and success in their respective sports. In the highly competitive and demanding world of sports, the mental aspect often becomes the differentiating factor between greatness and mediocrity. The ability to maintain composure under pressure, overcome setbacks, and consistently perform at a high level is dependent on an athlete's mental strength and mental preparedness.

These case studies collectively emphasize the significance of mental health support and psychological training in sports. By prioritizing mental well-being, athletes can enhance their performance, manage stress and anxiety, and develop the mental fortitude needed to excel in the face of challenges.

Sports organizations, coaches, and athletes themselves must recognize the importance of mental health and invest in mental training programs to optimize performance and overall well-being. Creating a positive and supportive team environment, providing access to sports psychologists, and promoting open conversations about mental health are essential steps toward nurturing athletes' mental health.

The case studies of these remarkable athletes serve as a testament to the profound impact of mental health and psychological skills in sports. Embracing and enhancing these aspects will not only elevate athletic performance but also contribute to the holistic development and well-being of athletes, ensuring sustained success and fulfillment throughout their sporting careers. The fusion of physical prowess and mental strength creates a winning formula that champions both on and off the field, leaving a lasting legacy in the world of sports.

www.ingramcontent.com/pod-product-compliance
Lightning Source LLC
LaVergne TN
LVHW040021070726
842759LV00026B/549